DREAM JOBS IN SPORTS PSYCHOLOGY

JESSICA SHAW

Rosen
YA

Published in 2018 by The Rosen Publishing Group, Inc.
29 East 21st Street, New York, NY 10010

Library of Congress Cataloging-in-Publication Data

Names: Shaw, Jessica, 1972– author.
Title: Dream Jobs in Sports Psychology / Jessica Shaw.
Description: New York : Rosen Publishing, 2018. | Series: Great
Careers in the Sports Industry | Includes bibliographical refer-
ences and index. | Audience: Grades 7–12.
Identifiers: LCCN 2017018659 | ISBN 9781538381441 (library
bound) | ISBN 9781508178644 (paperback)
Subjects: LCSH: Sports—Psychological aspects—Juvenile
literature. | Sports psychologists—Juvenile literature. | Sports—
Vocational guidance—Juvenile literature.
Classification: LCC GV706.4 .S523 2018 | DDC 796.023—dc23
LC record available at https://lccn.loc.gov/2017018659

Manufactured in China

CONTENTS

Austrian skydiver and BASE jumper Felix Baumgartner became the first person to break the speed of sound with his jump from 24 miles (39 km) above the earth's surface.

In 1986, at age sixteen, a young Austrian man named Felix Baumgartner went skydiving for the first time in his life. It was to be the first of many awe-inspiring aerial maneuvers for Baumgartner. Not long after that first dive, he joined the Austrian special forces' aerial competition team. Then, in 1988, he was hired by Red Bull to perform skydiving exhibitions. The thrill of aerial sports pushed him to continuously challenge himself. In 1999, he set a world BASE jumping record of more than 1,400 feet (427 meters). In 2003, he flew across the English Channel in a carbon-wing glider and a suit he designed himself. Always looking to push his limits, he jumped into Croatia's 623-foot (189-m) Marmet Cave in 2004. In all, Baumgartner has set fourteen world records in BASE jumping and inspired sky divers all around the world. His greatest achievement came in 2012, when he became the first person to break the speed of sound in free fall, jumping from the earth's stratosphere above New Mexico. For this daring stunt, he was carried twenty-four miles (thirty-nine kilometers) into the air by a sixty-story helium balloon. Then, wearing a specially designed space suit, oxygen tanks, and parachute rigs, he jumped out of the balloon and fell toward Earth at speeds of more than 800 miles (1,287 km) per hour. There had been only one other free fall jump of this magnitude, but Baumgartner was jumping from several miles higher than the previous record holder. There was no way to know if he would escape injury, or if he would even survive the fall. Baumgartner did survive...and promptly moved on to the challenge of racecar driving!

Someone like Baumgartner, with a seemingly bottomless supply of courage, motivation, physical strength, and mental toughness, might not seem like the type of person who would ever be in need of a sport psychologist. On the contrary, Baumgartner was not only daring, brave, and talented enough to accomplish many amazing feats, he was also smart and savvy enough to know when to seek help from a sport psychologist. As one might expect, there are many things that can go wrong during aerial stunts, and even one thing going wrong—a tear in a suit, a malfunctioning tank, a missed calculation—could quite possibly result in death. These unknown factors kept Baumgartner awake at night, and he sought out the help of an experienced sport psychologist, Mike Gervais. Working with Gervais gave Baumgartner the mental tools he needed to overcome his waves of fear and take a supersonic jump into the Guinness Book of World Records.

Sports psychology is an interdisciplinary field, meaning it is a field requiring a high level of competency in separate areas. Becoming a successful sport psychologist requires knowledge, skill, and training in the field of psychology, as well as an in-depth understanding and appreciation of sports and the intense training required of all athletes. Becoming a sport psychologist is a difficult, demanding pursuit that calls for academic excellence and many years of hard work, but it is an exciting, satisfying, lucrative field that is gaining in popularity. The stigma that was once attached to seeing a psychologist is giving way to the appreciation of a useful, beneficial field of study that gives athletes a mental edge.

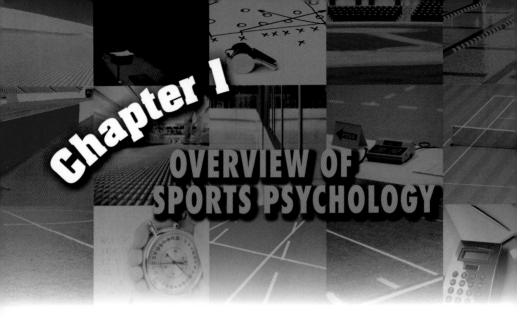

Chapter 1

OVERVIEW OF SPORTS PSYCHOLOGY

Many who envision a career helping others are drawn to the social sciences, and, specifically, to the field of psychology. There are many rewarding careers for psychologists and numerous areas of specialization. For those who happen to be passionate about both helping others and about sports, a specialization in sports psychology might be the perfect fit. Sports psychology is a branch of psychology that looks at the effects of sports—or other physically demanding endeavors—on an individual and attempts to improve their performance, using psychological strategies to foster a strong, healthy mindset. Since the earliest days of athletic competitions, athletes, coaches, and trainers have known that achieving success in any sport requires not only physical strength and skill, but also mental preparedness.

Likewise, to effectively maintain a successful career in sports—despite fame, notoriety, or setbacks— athletes need to stay grounded and mentally focused. Before the

Coaches have long been, and continue to be, a great source of support for athletes, even as sports psychologists gain in popularity.

field of sports psychology emerged, coaches, trainers, and athletes themselves were the only ones who could fill this gap and provide the necessary psychological support. This is no longer the case. Increasingly, sports psychologists are proving to be a crucial part of the modern day–training regimen for athletes in virtually every sport.

THE EVOLUTION OF SPORTS PSYCHOLOGY

The argument can be made that sports psychology has been around, informally, since the earliest athletic competitions. Friends, family members, and even other competitors who had something constructive to say before, during, or after an event played a role in an athlete's success. The first comment on performance, the first motivational words shouted during a competition, the first compliments paid to a victor—these were, in essence, the humblest beginnings of sports psychology.

Dr. Norman Triplett, a psychologist at Indiana University, conducted the first formal experiment in sports psychology. His theory was that cyclists would achieve faster times when competing against others versus cycling alone. In 1898, Triplett published his research findings, which proved his theory was correct. Improvement in performance because of the presence of others is a psychological effect known as social facilitation. Triplett's research paved the way for future sports psychologists and earned him an honorary historical distinction as the grandfather of sports psychology.

In 1918, a young graduate student named Coleman Griffith was studying psychology in sports. A few years later, after earning his PhD in psychology, Dr. Griffith began teaching a course on psychology and athletics at the University of Illinois. Then, in 1925, he opened a laboratory in the United States—the first of its kind—where he conducted numerous experiments and researched athletic performance over the next several years. He published many research papers and

A ROUGH START ON WRIGLEY FIELD

Dr. Coleman Griffith, the father of sports psychology, was also the first sport psychologist hired by a professional sports team. In 1937, he was offered a job by Philip K. Wrigley, the owner of the Chicago Cubs baseball team. Though this was a very important moment in the history of sports psychology, it turned out to be an unsuccessful first venture. The Cubs' team manager, Charlie Grimm, didn't think Griffith had anything

(continued on the next page)

Wrigley Field, home of the Chicago Cubs, opened in Chicago, Illinois, in 1914 and is the second-oldest Major League Baseball field in the United States.

(continued from the previous page)

to offer the team. In fact, Grimm openly mocked Griffith and instructed the players not to cooperate with him.

Grimm and Griffith continued to butt heads until Grimm was fired in 1938 and replaced by Gabby Hartnett. Unfortunately, Hartnett was no more open to Griffith's help than Grimm had been. In these early days before sports psychologists were recognized and valued, it was easy for a coach to take offense to someone else being hired to help the team improve. After all, up until that point, improving the team's performance was strictly the coach's job. By 1940, Griffith was fed up and left the team. Many baseball managers deemed the Cubs' trial run with a sport psychologist a failure, and it was quite some time before another team hired one.

two textbooks on sports psychology, *Psychology and Coaching* in 1926 and *Psychology and Athletics* in 1928. He was also the first psychologist to work for a professional sports team. Dr. Griffith is widely regarded as the founder and father of sports psychology.

HELP WANTED: JOB OPPORTUNITIES IN SPORTS PSYCHOLOGY

As the name suggests, sports psychologists are professionals who often work directly with athletes. In fact,

Competitive swimmers are just one of many types of athletes who often enlist the help of a sport psychologist to perform at their very best.

working with athletes to improve their performance is the job description most commonly associated with the title of sport psychologist. In actuality, though, the field of sports psychology is quite broad and offers a multitude of career paths. There are job opportunities for sports psychologists who want to work with individual athletes or with sports teams, those who want to work in the corporate arena, those who enjoy research and teaching, and even those who would like to pursue a military career.

Sports psychologists are increasingly being consulted by all types of athletes in nearly every sport imaginable. They are often hired by athletic teams or schools, but sometimes they maintain their own private practice and are hired for consultation by individuals or teams on an as-needed basis. It has become common practice for sports psychologists to be hired to work with athletes and entire teams in the more well-known, well-broadcast sports like football, basketball, baseball, soccer, golf, and tennis, but sports psychologists are also at work with those competing in a variety of other events, at both the amateur and

Runners must be in top shape both physically and psychologically to perform well. They must be able to tune out distractions all around as they head to the starting line.

professional level. Dancers, bowlers, racecar drivers, swimmers, runners, weight lifters, skaters, hockey players, and any number of Olympians-in-training are just a few examples. Many highly successful athletes have sought the help of a sport psychologist to further their career, with golfers and tennis players among the most frequent consumers of sports psychologists' services. Golfing legends Tiger Woods, Annika Sorenstam, Greg Norman, and Jack Nicklaus represent a small sampling of the estimated three hundred plus professional golfers known to have consulted with sports psychologists.

The mindset of competitive athletes is one of focus and drive to be the best. Just as athletes push themselves to be at the top of the field, so do many in the competitive corporate world. Sports psychologists may choose to pursue a job within human resources or consulting for private companies, helping individual employees meet fitness goals, overcome performance anxiety, or develop a plan for a healthy lifestyle. More and more companies are offering this type of consultation to their employees. The companies that do so benefit because employees who are mentally and physically fit miss fewer workdays and experience a higher level of satisfaction, which tends to keep them with the company longer. Team-building exercises in the workplace are very popular and another potential avenue for a sport psychologist. Sports psychologists also develop and implement exercise programs for rehabilitation centers, hospitals, prisons, or other institutions. Sports psychologists with an entrepreneurial spirit might choose to own and manage their own fitness facility or provide training to other fitness professionals. There are many rewarding career tracks for sports psychologists to pursue, outside of professional sports arenas and training centers.

For sports psychologists who find they have a passion for teaching, there is a growing need for qualified professionals who can help other prospective sports psychologists fulfill the academic requirements. As the field continues to expand and evolve, more schools are offering courses and degree programs in sports psychology. Some high schools are now offering classes in sports psychology, and if the trend continues, there will be an increased demand for teachers at this level. The majority of teaching jobs are at colleges and universities, where there are often research opportunities as well. At first glance, a job in research might seem to pale in comparison to working directly with athletes, but imagine inspiring others to excel in the field and helping to shape the future of sports psychology, developing and honing new psychological methods to maximize the success of athletes for years to come. It is easy

It is vital for all members of the military to have access to top-notch psychological services in order to face the multitude of challenges military service brings.

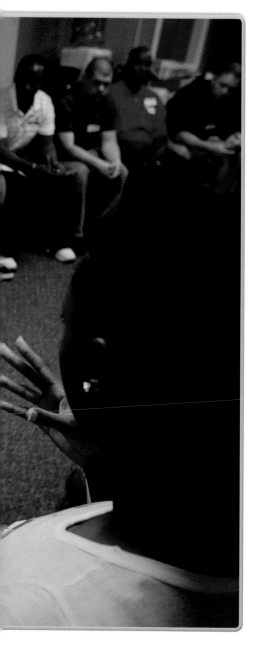

to understand why sports psychologists involved in research and teaching find it to be a worthwhile, meaningful experience. Another benefit of choosing this career path is potentially having summers off and not having to worry about traveling with an athlete or team.

Sports psychologists are also in demand in the military. Soldiers face physical and mental challenges that can be much more difficult than the obstacles and setbacks athletes face. In the military, a loss can mean the loss of a life as opposed to just losing a game or placing last in an event. A soldier's well-being is in large part dependent upon mental preparedness and toughness. Those in the military who suffer the loss of a fellow soldier, experience a traumatic encounter on the battlefield, or sustain an injury are especially susceptible to depression or post-traumatic stress disorder (PTSD). The families of soldiers also endure hardships and can greatly benefit from professional psychological services. For all of these reasons, the role of sports psychologists in the military is perhaps the most important of all.

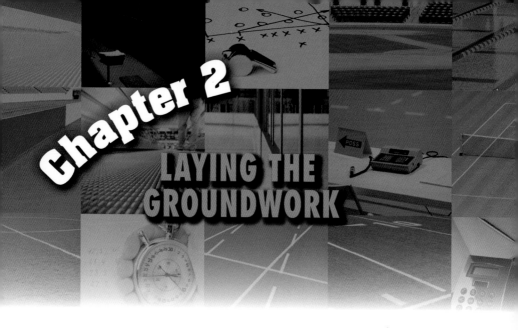

Chapter 2

LAYING THE GROUNDWORK

S tudents who think about what they can do during their high school years to ensure acceptance to a reputable college are one step ahead. High school students who have an idea of a career track they would like to pursue and spend some time researching their field of interest to find ways to work toward that goal are many steps ahead. This forethought and planning is beneficial in so many ways, and even more so for those interested in a field that is very competitive, such as sports psychology.

IN THE CLASSROOM

Maintaining a high grade point average in high school is especially important for students hoping to attend a top-notch college. All universities have certain admission standards that a prospective student must meet to gain acceptance. These standards are specific to each institution,

Hard work in high school is the first step for students hoping to pursue a college degree in a challenging field such as sports psychology.

but usually include a minimum score on standardized tests such as the ACT or SAT, graduation from high school with an acceptable grade point average, and, often, participation in extracurricular activities and/or community service hours. Overall, esteemed colleges are hoping for hard-working, motivated, responsible, well-rounded applicants.

Aside from establishing excellent study skills and maintaining high grades, care should be taken in choosing high school classes. Many classes taken in high school are required as part of the degree plan, but there are still a considerable number of options for students to customize their high school plan. Choosing to take an advanced placement,

Developing strong communication skills is an important goal to work toward in high school. Psychologists must be excellent communicators to work effectively with clients.

accelerated, or honors level course rather than a basic course is a good choice for many students, as long as they are willing to put in the necessary effort in the class. These classes require more hours of studying and often involve more complex projects and assignments, but they are impressive achievements to have listed on a high school transcript. Advanced classes are typically weighted, meaning, for example, an A earned in an advanced class is worth more than an A earned in a regular class when calculating grade point averages. A certain number of elective classes are also required in high school. For those interested in sports psychology, it is important to choose social sciences as electives, when possible. Social sciences include classes such as psychology, sociology, humanities, anthropology, geography, and economics. Social science classes focus on society and the relationships between people. These types of classes lay the groundwork for a future career in sports psychology.

Sports psychologists need to excel at communicating, both verbally and in writing, so classes such as speech or creative writing are excellent choices. Biology, statistics, and math are important components of psychological research, so these, too, are beneficial. Lastly, when thinking about high school curriculum, consider taking dual credit courses, if offered. There are often many to choose from, including classes that fall under the social science category.

GETTING AHEAD WITH DUAL CREDIT

Not so long ago, the only classes students could take in high school were high school classes. Many new options have become available, though, and more and more high schools have forged partnerships with local community colleges to offer dual credit classes. They are called dual credit classes because students earn both high school credit that counts toward their graduation requirements, as well as college credit that counts toward the hours required for a college degree. These classes offer an excellent opportunity for high school students to get a jump start on their college coursework and can also help a student narrow down which fields are of interest before beginning college and declaring a major. An added bonus is that there is typically no course fee for these classes when taken as part of the high school curriculum, only the cost of the college textbook. This means a savings of potentially thousands of dollars, if several of these classes are taken in high school. In some instances, students can even begin college classified as a sophomore rather than as a freshman because of the number of dual credit classes they took in high school. One less year of college means a huge savings in both time and money invested and puts students that much closer to embarking on a successful career.

Another option well worth exploring in high school is an internship. Some high schools offer excellent internship programs that match students up with professionals, according to career interests. For example, specialized areas of internships may include business, government, technology, manufacturing, or any number of careers in wellness and health services, such as nursing, physical therapy, or fitness. A student interested in sports psychology might be paired with a coach, a physical therapist working to rehabilitate athletes, a fitness trainer, or even an actual sport psychologist. Students usually receive a grade, just as they would in class, but they spend part of their day off campus, in a professional setting, observing, assisting, and learning more about their chosen field of interest. In this way, a student is able to see first-hand what a certain job entails, and this experience can motivate the student to work even harder toward that goal. Likewise, this type of experience might also lead a student to decide that a certain career is not a good fit. Either way, the experience of interning is a worthwhile one that looks great on college admission applications and helps narrow down career paths. In addition to high school internships that take place during the school year, there are also many colleges that offer camps and programs during the summer that are geared specifically toward high school students interested in pursuing psychology. Sports psychology is a competitive field, so any experience that offers students an ad-

Working with a coach or trainer while in high school is a great way to gain experience and learn about motivational techniques.

vantage over other college applicants vying for an education in sports psychology merits serious consideration.

ON THE FIELD

Gaining practical, hands-on experience in sports is very important for students interested in sports psychology. In order to one day work with athletes, it is essential to understand what it takes to compete in sports and to be familiar with the ups and downs that are commonplace for all athletes. Aspiring sports psychologists do not need to be sports prodigies with rooms full of trophies, but the more experience gained and time spent participating in sports, the better they will be able to relate to athletes as a psychologist.

Participating in high school sports offers students first-hand experience in the challenges and rewards athletes face.

To be effective, sports psychologists need to understand the psychological strategies that are the most motivational to an athlete, just as good coaches do. The mindset that successful leaders embrace is sometimes referred to as a "coaching mentality," as opposed to a strictly managerial or boss mentality. Using a coaching mentality means realizing the importance of keeping fun in the game and relating to players on a positive and personal level to gain their trust and bond with them, whereas taking a strictly boss-like approach usually only serves to alienate players. There are many ways for high school students to begin learning about this positive psychological approach used by coaches and sports psychologists.

The most obvious way to gain sports experience while in high school is to play one or more sports. Playing a sport is a fun way to gain experience, but it is certainly not the only way. Some sports-loving students might try out but not make the team. Others might have physical limitations that prevent them from playing a sport, even though they very much want to be involved in high school sports. There are also some who might not feel ready to try out for a team, and would like to learn more about a sport for a while before trying out. In all of these situations, becoming a team manager is a great option to consider. Team managers are important members of high school sports teams. They help with a multitude of things, including equipment management, time keeping, assisting with

THE WIDE WORLD OF SPORTS

Being a high school athlete might mean participating in sports such as football, basketball, baseball, soccer, or tennis, but it could also mean participating in lesser-known events. Every sport requires dedication and skill, however not all of them require abs of steel or bulging biceps. There are many alternatives for those who don't think they are a good fit for the more mainstream high school sports. Activities such as archery, golf, racquetball, ice skating, rowing, cycling, rock climbing, and mountain biking are a few of the fun, challenging alternatives for those looking to gain experience in the world of sports. Some of these activities are offered through larger high school athletic departments, but local sports clubs or organizations are also valuable resources for anyone interested in learning a new sport and becoming part of a team. Involvement in a sport of any kind is beneficial for students hoping to pursue a sports-related career such as sports psychology, and involvement in a variety of sports is an excellent way to gain experience and relate to a wide range of athletes.

injured athletes, rosters, water coolers, and communication with athletes' parents. Team managers have a perfect opportunity to learn more about a sport, be a part of a team, gain insight into coaching methods, and bond with players and coaches. High school team managers often go on to play on a team or become a sports team manager in college, both impressive achievements for aspiring sports psychologists.

Another way to gain valuable sports experience while in high school is volunteering with local youth sports organizations or clubs. A good way to find out about these types of opportunities is through a local community center. High school coaches or school counselors might also be good sources of information for sports-related volunteer opportunities. Most communities have youth sports organizations for football, soccer, basketball, baseball, and more. Even if there is not an active posting asking for help, interested high school students should not hesitate to reach out and offer their services as a volunteer. These organizations are usually non-profit and are always on the lookout for teen volunteers to serve as role models and mentors for their young players. Often, teen volunteers are even called upon to be assistant coaches. Young kids who are getting their start in sports look up to "big kids" as coaches. This is not only a wonderful opportunity to gain experience and work toward a career in sports psychology, it is also a great way to make a difference in individual children's lives.

Finding a sports-related job is a win-win situation for students. It is an opportunity to gain valuable experience in a sport and earn some money at the same time.

Students interested in a sports-related career such as sports psychology can gain valuable experience volunteering or gaining employment with a local sports organization.

Baseball enthusiasts can earn money as umpires for their local youth baseball league. Local youth soccer, basketball, and football leagues sometimes hire teens to referee games. Organizations like YMCA or a Boys and Girls Club offer job opportunities in after-school sports and recreational programs. Some YMCA locations have an indoor pool and hire lifeguards year-round, and those with an outdoor pool hire lifeguards for the summer months. Summer employment as a sports camp counselor is another way to enjoy a fun, sports-related experience while earning a paycheck. Parks and recreation departments are an excellent resource for researching summer camp jobs. Most colleges also offer summer sports programs, and may be open to hiring teenagers. It is a good idea to check into potential positions well in advance, as interviews and hiring often take place weeks or even months before jobs begin. All of these are excellent opportunities in sports that could very well lead to future or ongoing employment as well as opportunities to make connections and network with athletic trainers, coaches, and other sports professionals.

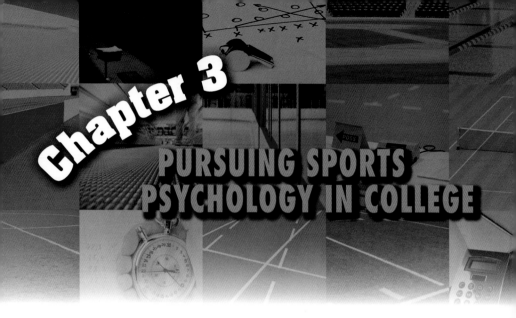

Chapter 3

PURSUING SPORTS PSYCHOLOGY IN COLLEGE

For most major courses of study in college, the class requirements and degree outline are fairly straightforward and serve as a road map for students. This is not necessarily the case for students pursuing sports psychology. The academic requirements and practical experience that future sports psychologists need may require some creative thinking, extra motivation, and an abundance of ambition.

ACADEMIC ROADMAP

Since sports psychology is an interdisciplinary field and a relatively new professional career track, most universities do not offer an undergraduate degree in sports psychology. Likewise, not many universities offer a graduate program in sports psychology either. Those colleges that do offer a designated sports psychology major and/or graduate program are few and far between and have high

As high school graduation draws near, students should carefully research colleges to find the right fit and, if possible, tour them in person.

standards for admission. This is where early planning and research done in high school can really pay off. Attending a school that offers a sports psychology track is an excellent choice, but doing so is not an option for every student starting college who is interested in sports psychology. Rest assured, attending a school that offers a sports psychology degree program is not the only path to becoming a sport psychologist.

Choosing which colleges to apply to is an important decision for every high school graduate and even more so for students who are pursuing a specialized career. It is essential that sports psychology students seek out a school that has excellent academic standing, a renowned psychology department, and a solid sports program. Some undergraduate schools in the United States that offer a major, minor, or concentration in sports psychology include: Drexel University, National University, Fredonia State University, University of Evansville, University of Utah, Western Washington University, University of Northern Iowa, and West Virginia University. Alternatively, some schools offer a closely related major, such as the psychosocial kinesiology major at Texas Christian University.

First and foremost, students pursuing sports psychology need to un-

Beautiful and historic Woodburn Hall is part of West Virginia University's (WVU) downtown campus. WVU offers both undergraduate and graduate degrees in exercise and sports psychology.

derstand that becoming a psychologist requires, at minimum, a master's degree, regardless of area of specialization within the field. This means that a minimum of six years of college is to be expected. A bachelor's degree is a four-year degree, and though students can graduate in four years with a bachelor's degree in psychology, this is different from actually being a psychologist. There are a limited number of colleges that offer a bachelor's degree in sports psychology, so most students will have to choose a bachelor's degree in psychology, or in a sports-related field such as kinesiology or exercise science as a starting point. In addition to fulfilling the core requirements for all bachelor's degrees such as English, history, math, and political science classes, students pursuing sports psychology will want to choose elective classes that support their career track. In other words, since most sports psychology students are not majoring in a specific four-year sports psychology curriculum, those who are majoring in psychology will want to choose electives that are sports or exercise related. Conversely, those majoring in sports or exercise would be wise to choose psychology courses as electives. A bachelor's degree is just the beginning for a sport psychologist, followed by at least two more years in graduate school to earn a master's degree in psychology. If attending one of the schools that offers a graduate program in sports psychology is not feasible, there are colleges that offer an advanced degree in counseling or clinical psychology with a concentration in sports psychology. These programs offer a foundation in understanding and treating psychological disturbances and typically include coursework in the physiological or biomechanical bases of sport. Coupled with practical, hands-on sports experience, this is a perfectly acceptable route for a future sport psychologist to take. Applying for sports or psychology related work-study programs or internships is also an important step to take. In college, as students draw closer to embarking on a career as a sport psychologist, these types of experiences are even more important than in high school. A student's department chair can be instrumental in helping arrange internships that offer excellent experience within a given field of study.

After obtaining a bachelor's degree, it is time to find a good graduate program. Sports psychology graduate programs may include advanced coursework in statistics, coaching, sport biomechanics, anatomy and physiology, psychology, research, and motivation as they apply to sports performance. Graduate work usually also includes a thesis paper on an advanced topic related to sports psychology. For students who find themselves at a graduate school that offers only introductory courses

Students pursuing sports psychology at the collegiate level must be diligent in maintaining a high grade point average and committed to seeking out additional opportunities for learning about the field.

related to sports psychology, it is essential to seek out opportunities to enhance their education, so as to closely resemble that of a graduate program in sports psychology. One way to do this is to approach the department chair and ask if it is possible to take independent study or independent research classes related to the field. As the names denote, these types of classes involve working independently, but also working closely with a professional, such as a coach at the university, or being involved in research under a professor, to supplement coursework. Upon the completion of all academic requirements to earn a master's degree in sports psychology—or in some cases, a master's degree in psychology—graduates might want to continue on to earn their PhD. They will also most likely want to work toward certification with the Association for Applied Sports psychology (AASP) or the American Board of Sports psychology (ABSP). Though certification with the AASP or ABSP is not required to be a sport psychologist, it is highly recommended as it improves marketability and is a prerequisite of some employers.

The American Psychological Association (APA) has a division specifically devoted to exercise and sports psychology. It is called Division 47, and its purpose is to further understanding, promote research, and provide networking opportunities, mentoring, and information about the field of exercise and sports psychology. Members include sports psychology service providers, scientists, and researchers. Division 47 also offers student memberships, and this is highly recommended for all students interested in this exciting field. For a nominal fee, the student membership provides numerous perks, including regular newsletters and journals with the most up-to-date industry news and information, eligibility for student awards, opportunities to serve as a student editorial reviewer for publications or as a student member or representative on a Division 47

ALL ABOUT CERTIFICATION

In a growing, competitive field such as sports psychology, education, experience, and credentials are all vital to success. Professional certification as a sport psychologist, though not mandatory in all cases, is a very good idea. Certification is obtained through the Association for Applied Sports psychology (AASP) or the American Board of Sports psychology (ABSP). For AASP certification, applicants must hold a graduate degree, demonstrate their knowledge in the field, and have several hundred hours of experience. Those with a master's degree are eligible for a provisional certification, while those with a doctoral degree can obtain a standard certification. A doctoral degree is required for ABSP certification, as well as a current license to practice or a considerable amount of research and/or publications, passage of an examination, and experience in the field. Clearly, it is not easy to achieve professional certification, but sports psychologists who are certified will stand out when applying for coveted positions. Depending on the employer, sometimes only those sports psychologists who have attained professional certification are considered for a job opening. It is easy to see how an applicant's professional certification—or lack thereof—can make all the difference when trying to land a dream job.

committee, and reduced fees for attending the APA Annual Convention.

ATHLETIC COMPONENT

Staying involved in sports is critical in college, even as the demands of classes and homework mount. Just as in high school, there are a variety of ways to expand upon sports proficiency and knowledge. Equally important is making valuable connections with professionals in sports. Many of the options available to high school students are still excellent choices for college students pursuing sports psychology. These include assisting

Being involved in youth sports is a rewarding and beneficial experience. Learning to relate to and mentor young athletes is an essential skill set for future sports psychologists.

or coaching youth sports teams, working at sports summer camps, and playing sports. Once in college, there will also be the chance to become involved in collegiate sports teams. Making contacts within the school's athletic department is a great first step and one that will hopefully lead to introductions to different members of the coaching staff and/or school athletes. It is a good idea to inquire about volunteer opportunities in the athletic department, and students should let it be known that they are pursuing a degree in sports psychology. Playing a sport, whether at the varsity, club, or intramural level, or assisting with a team in some way is a valuable experience and one that every student can achieve.

Some students may have already benefitted from participating in an internship or a work-study program in high school. In college, there are usually more and a wider variety of opportunities of this kind. Internships may be available in physical/sports rehabilitation centers, training rooms, or in various positions within the athletic department. Often, these opportunities are not advertised and must be sought out.

College students will have even more employment opportunities than high school students. A college's office of student affairs will usually offer career counseling, job listings, and help with job placement for current

COLLEGE SPORTS— VARSITY, CLUB, OR INTRAMURAL?

There are several options for college students who want to play sports. There are varsity, club, or intramural teams that might be a good fit, depending on a student's interests and qualifications. Varsity teams typically represent their college and play in games against other colleges. The team receives funding from the school's athletic fund. The players on these teams are usually—though not always—students who played and excelled in high school sports. There are collegiate sports organizations that oversee competition in varsity sports. Play is divided into three levels: Division I, Division II, and Division III, with Division I being the largest and most competitive. Students who don't make a varsity team or don't want to compete in sports with the intensity of varsity-level play might choose a club team. Club teams are organized and run by the students themselves, with teams from different colleges playing each other. Games are still very competitive, and there is a considerable time commitment, but not in comparison to varsity sports. Yet another option is playing intramural sports. Intramural leagues are set up by colleges and offer virtually any interested student a chance to play sports. These leagues are designed to be fun and informal, with teams from the same college playing each other. Sometimes there are different levels of play offered, allowing students to choose which level is ideal for their abilities.

There are many opportunities to play sports in college. Involvement in sports is beneficial for sports psychology students, whether playing on a college team or just in a recreational league.

and former students. This is a good place to begin a job search while in college. A career placement adviser meets with students to learn about their previous job experience, their major in college, and the types of job opportunities the student is looking for. Employers regularly contact college career placement offices looking for students to employ. The career placement adviser is able to put them in contact with students who are a good match for their line of work. For students who attend college close to home, previous employers or coaches from high school are good resources for seeking sports-related job leads. Making and maintaining good contacts in the sports world may seem like a recurring theme, and it is. Professional contacts are important in all walks of life, but the sports industry is very interconnected, and making a good impression on all coaches, trainers, and teammates over the years can be worth its weight in gold in a field like sports psychology.

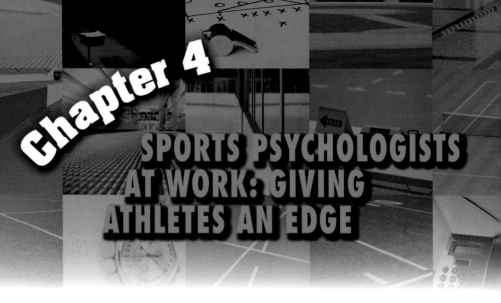

Chapter 4

SPORTS PSYCHOLOGISTS AT WORK: GIVING ATHLETES AN EDGE

Responsibilities of sports psychologists working with athletes may vary according to their employer or place of employment, but day-to-day duties typically include similar tasks and challenges. On a regular basis,

Sport psychologist David Scott talks with West Indies cricket player Tino Best. It is becoming common practice for athletes to consult with sports psychologists to help improve their performance.

most sports psychologists who work with athletes find themselves developing detailed strategies to help improve performance or overcome mental obstacles; meeting with individual athletes or teams to implement these strategies; offering insight, advice, relaxation exercises, and counseling services; and meeting with coaches or team managers to discuss needs, observations, or potential changes in strategy.

HELPING ALL LEVELS OF ATHLETES

There are two types of sports psychologists who work with athletes. Clinical sports psychologists focus on diagnosing and treating mental health issues that are common to athletes. These issues include performance anxiety, eating disorders, and depression. Applied sports psychologists focus on motivation and mental conditioning techniques that help athletes achieve peak performance. It is important to point out that an athlete may need applied sports psychology emphasis one week and clinical sports psychology support the next. Often, one licensed, well-trained sport psychologist can provide both clinical and applied sports psychology services to clients, and this is beneficial for athletes who may already have a close, trusting relationship with their team psychologist and be hesitant to see a new one.

Many collegiate sports teams consult a sport psychologist. Some teams from large schools, such as the

VISUALIZING SUCCESS

Many factors contribute to an athlete's successful performance. Physical condition, training, weather conditions, mental state, and any number of unknown influences can all play a role. One common technique top athletes have learned through working with sports psychologists is visualization. Visualization is a multisensory process in which athletes focus on a detailed mental image of the events leading up to, and including, their performance. They visualize and imagine everything from the crowds of people, cameras, air temperature, and lighting conditions to the feelings of their muscles tightening and the butterflies in their stomach as they mentally go through their performance. Imagining every last detail—including possible distractions—allows them to prepare for every possibility. Nicole Detling, a sport psychologist with the United States Olympic team, tells athletes that the more they imagine the entire experience beforehand, the better it's going to be. According to a 2014 article by the Huffington Post, former Olympic runner Marty Liquori used visualization throughout his career and said of the technique, "I have always believed, if you want to be a champion, you will have to win every race in your mind 100 times before you win it in real life that last time." Many elite athletes use this technique consistently and believe that visualizing their success indeed makes success more likely.

Florida State Seminoles, the 2014 NCAA football champions, keep a sport psychologist on staff. Seminoles' head coach, Jimbo Fisher, realized that sports psychologists were not only useful during troubled times: even if a player wasn't struggling with a mental block or setback, that didn't mean there was no room for improvement. He believed in putting as much of an emphasis on mental conditioning as physical in the Seminoles' football program. Given the team's successful record, clearly this strategy worked well for them.

After winning the 2014 men's hockey championship, the Union College Hockey captain, Mat Bodie, acknowledged the extent to which their team psychologist helped them get the win in a 2014 *Sports psychology Institute Northwest* article, "Just one shift at a time. This is the biggest game of our lives, hands down, but you've got to treat it like any other game. It was tough… it was real tough to keep that mindset, but with our sport psychologist we were able to get that done."

Though sports psychology is now a recognized and respected field, not all colleges have the funds to keep a sport psychologist on staff. Many schools use sports psychologists on a contractual, as-needed basis. For instance, a sport psychologist may be hired to meet with a player or a team for a certain length of time or a certain number of sessions during especially stressful times, such as when an athlete or team is about to play in a crucial game, after the loss of a player or coach, or when a player is recovering from a major injury.

Sports psychologists who have a full-time position with a collegiate team have the benefit of getting to know each of the players on a team intimately. Knowing their individual personalities, their strengths and weaknesses, and the different stressors that might trigger self-doubt or anger is especially helpful when working toward the goal of helping the team improve overall performance. Likewise, having an ongoing, up-close look at the way the players function as a team, both in practice and during games, helps a sport psychologist determine how best to motivate the team and what advice to offer the coaching staff. The work environment may include an office, but is often right down on the playing field or in the locker room alongside coaches, including travelling with the team to away games. During off-season, the work doesn't end. Athletes are expected to stay in good shape year-round, and this includes maintaining a positive outlook and competitive mindset during periods of conditioning and training. Landing a position with a collegiate team is not easy, as there are a limited number of colleges that keep sports psychologists on staff, but for those who are flexible, willing to travel, and motivated to rise to the top in

Sports psychologists work with athletes both on and off the field, helping them to stay physically and mentally fit, recover from injuries, and maintain a healthy lifestyle, even during the off-season.

their field, becoming a collegiate-level sport psychologist is a worthwhile goal.

While working for a collegiate team as a sport psychologist is a much-coveted position, doing so for a professional team is perhaps an even more enviable position. At the professional level, many individual athletes as well as teams consistently work with a sport psychologist. The pressure on professional athletes is even greater than the pressure on college athletes because their success or failure on the field, track, slope, court, or golf course, or in the pool or ring is directly tied to their paycheck and job security. That same pressure is felt by the coaches and team owners as well, since their team's performance has a direct impact on their job and income. On a positive note, the budget for a professional athlete or team is typically bigger than for collegiate teams, and as sports psychologists have gained acceptance and a loyal following in the sports world, it is not uncommon for a team psychologist's salary to be included as part of that budget. The work environment for these psychologists is similar to collegiate sports psychologists, but in most cases involves more travel, depending on the sport and the length of its season. Psychologists who help individuals or teams achieve success at this level quickly become known as key players in the world of professional sports.

Perhaps the most prestigious of all employment opportunities for a sport psychologist is helping an Olympic athlete or team go for the gold for their country. The thrill of assisting in the development of a world-class athletic performance, culminating in millions of viewers tuning in, cheering for their respective countries and athletes, is a dream come true for some sports psychologists. Most countries now take numerous psychologists with them to the Olympic Games. At the 2014 Sochi Winter Olympics, the Canadian team brought eight psychologists, the Norwegians brought three, and the United States brought nine. According to Luke Bodensteiner, executive vice president of the United States Ski and Snowboard Association, many nations are now using more psychologists than they used to, thanks in large part to the US team's success over the years with sports psychologists.

The amount of pressure on Olympic athletes is hard to fathom. It goes beyond striving to make their school proud, keep their job, or secure their paycheck. The hopes and dreams of their entire home country rest squarely on Olympians' shoulders. It goes without saying that athletes with such an intense level of scrutiny and strain upon them greatly benefit from working with a sport psychologist. It takes years of training and preparation for an athlete to even have a chance at qualifying to compete in the Olympics, with many ups and downs along the way, such as injuries, anxiety, and other physical or psychological factors. Once the Olympic Games are over, it's not easy street for the athletes. There are tough challenges to contend with whether or not an Olympian goes home with a medal. The help of a sport psychologist after the Olympic Games is arguably just as important as beforehand.

Sports psychologists working with Olympians or Olympic teams can expect to travel extensively to qualifying meets or games in the years leading up to the Olympics. Then, for those athletes who qualify and their

The 2016 Olympic Games took place in Rio de Janeiro. Athletes and teams from many different countries brought sports psychologists with them to the games.

entourage of coaches, assistants, and psychologists, there will be the trip and competition of a lifetime. There is nothing typical about a workday at this level of competition, either for the athlete or the psychologist. At any given moment, an athlete might need more than a coach's pep talk about strategy, a trainer's bandage and ice pack, a teammate's hug, or a publicist's advice about speaking to a news crew. The sport psychologist is there to bridge every gap, whether the athlete needs to be tough in working through physical pain, emotionally strong after a disappointing performance, or mentally aggressive in facing a great opponent, there are specific psychological techniques—mental skills training techniques—that can help. One example is cognitive behavioral therapy (CBT). This approach recognizes that the way an individual perceives a situation is more likely to influence their reaction than the situation itself. In other words, if a diver who recently hit her head is suddenly convinced she is going to hit her head again when going off the diving board, it will not help her simply to explain the small chance of that happening again. In her mind, she is afraid it will happen. Her fear, if not controlled, will increase the likelihood of her making a mistake, and the reality of her skill level and the small chance of it happening again will not help her dismiss the fear. Instead, a sport psychologist using CBT would use any number of mental exercises, such as role playing, meditation, or imagery, to help her diminish the negative, fearful thoughts.

Olympians who have been dealt the blow of suffering a serious injury have both physical and mental challenges to overcome if they are to compete again. A sport psychologist helps these athletes work through the various stages of shock and grief and ultimately make the difficult decision to either attempt a comeback or retire from the sport. Win or lose, Olympic athletes face many stressors and greatly benefit from the guidance of a trained psychologist.

PLANNING BEYOND THE GAMES

With all the planning that goes into setting a goal as ambitious as competing in the Olympics, athletes might not stop to think about what will happen when the Games are over. Going back to a seemingly ordinary day-to-day life is difficult for elite athletes who are used to pushing themselves to the limit and being in the limelight with adrenaline coursing through their veins. This post-Olympic swing of emotion can often result in depression as athletes try to adjust to "normal" life again.

"Think about the rollercoaster ride prior to the Olympics, and just how fast and hectic that mad dash is," said Scott Goldman, director of the Performance Psychology Center at the University of Michigan, in a 2016 article in the Atlantic. "This ninety-mile-per-hour or hundred-mile-per-hour ride comes to a screeching halt the second the Olympics are over."

Olympic swimmer Allison Schmitt won five medals and set a world record in the 2012 Games in London, yet in the weeks and months that followed, she found herself sinking into a deep depression. Her USA teammate Michael Phelps faced a similar period of post-Olympic blues. Fortunately, both swimmers sought help and overcame their depression, but many successful athletes have the misconception that they have no right to be depressed, or that they should be tough enough to handle it on their own. Clinical sport psychologist

(continued on the next page)

(continued from the previous page)

Kristin Keim suggests athletes' ability to avoid depression lies in their readiness to build a new post-competition identity.

Olympians who identify themselves solely as an athlete—a swimmer, a skater, a gymnast—have the toughest time adjusting. It's vitally important that Olympic athletes develop a plan for post-Olympic life. Those who achieved or surpassed their personal goals in the Olympic Games can go from icon to ordinary status quickly when the hype subsides. Those who did not perform as well as they had hoped may be haunted by a feeling of "what could have been." Both scenarios are psychologically daunting. Sports psychologists can make all the difference for athletes before, during, and after the Olympics.

TOP SPORTS PSYCHOLOGISTS

Ninety minutes before every game, former Creighton University basketball star Doug McDermott would meet with the university's sport psychologist, Jack Stark, to take part in a series of visual relaxation exercises. This routine between McDermott and Stark continued from freshman year to senior year, with McDermott recognized for outstanding performance several times, including as the 2014 NCAA Men's Basketball Player of the Year.

McDermott discovered at a young age what many athletes and coaches have come to realize. The physical performance on the court or field is only part of the battle; the psychological factor can tip the scales. Athletes must be talented and hardworking to be competitive in any given sport, but there seems to be little doubt these days that a good sport psychologist can give an athlete enough of a mental edge to push them beyond *good* to *great*.

Beginning in the early 1900s with the work of Dr. Coleman Griffith, the father of sports psychology and the first psychologist to work for a sports team, psychologists have slowly but surely made themselves indispensable in the world of sports. Today, there are many sports psychologists who are renowned and sought after by all types of athletes.

Alan Goldberg has made a name for himself in sports psychology by focusing on youth sports over the span of several decades. He specializes in helping young people overcome common fears in sports and push themselves to reach their potential. He has worked with junior athletes in virtually every sport and at all levels and with coaches and parents to ensure their relationships on and off the field are healthy, positive ones. Dr. Goldberg writes for several national publications such as *Swimming World* and *Collegiate Baseball*. His successful career shines light on the fact that there is a need for sports psychologists who work

In earlier Olympic Games, athletes were solely dependent upon input from their coaches and teammates for motivation and help in improving performance.

with young athletes just starting out and that early psychological guidance is an ideal scenario for our future athletes.

Some sports psychologists were successful athletes before they began a career helping others to be successful athletes. One such psychologist is Dr. Caroline Silby, a former nationally ranked skater who was sent to the 1984 Olympic trials. Her personal experience as an elite athlete combined with her rigorous academic pursuit of psychology has brought her recognition as one of the top sports psychologists in the field. She has appeared on numerous television programs and is the author of *Games Girls Play: Understanding and Guiding Young Female Athletes*. Dr. JoAnn Dahlkoetter is also a highly regarded sport psychologist who is a former athlete. She is a past winner of the San Francisco Marathon who also took second place in the Hawaii Ironman Triathlon. Like Dr. Silby, Dr. Dahlkoetter's experience as a world-class athlete gave her great perspective as she pursued her education and eventual career as a leading sport psychologist. She has worked with many Olympic-level athletes and is the author of *Olympic Thinking*, a book that lays out a step-by-step plan for achieving sharp mental focus and peak performance.

Other successful sports psychologists have risen to the top of their field without jaw-dropping feats of athleticism. Dr. Terry Orlick earned his PhD

Sigmund Freud was an early pioneer in the field of psychiatry. He is known as the father of psychoanalysis, an effective, dialog-based technique that helps patients overcome psychological issues.

in 1972, and over an impressive decades-long career, he has worked with thousands of Olympians and professional athletes. He is considered a leading authority on achieving excellence and helping athletes perform at the highest possible level. Dr. Orlick is the author of several books, including *In Pursuit of Excellence* and *Embracing Your Potential*, and started a website called the Zone of Excellence dedicated to helping people unlock their potential. Dr. John F. Murray is another well-known name in sports psychology. He was the first to introduce the idea of scoring mental performance using the Mental Performance Index, a tool he developed to help analyze football teams' performances. In reference to the famous psychologist Sigmund Freud, Dr. Murray has been called "The Freud of Football." He has worked with a variety of top athletes and is author of the book *Smart Tennis: How to Play and Win the Mental Game.*

These are just a few of the sports psychologists who have achieved great respect and notoriety while managing highly successful and fulfilling careers. Their contributions are considerable, impressive, and inspirational for anyone hoping to follow in their footsteps. Sports psychologists at the top of their field get to enjoy a job they are passionate about, and often become as sought after themselves as the most elite athletes on their client lists.

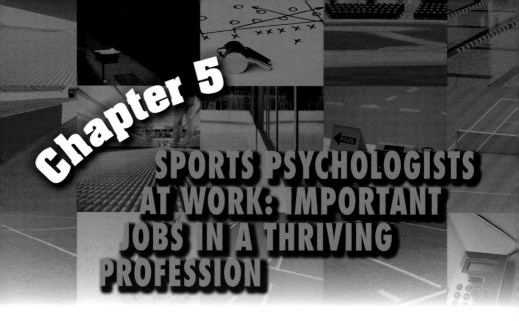

Not all sports psychologists work with athletes or sports teams. There are several other interesting options to consider in this growing field, including some that don't require being licensed as a psychologist. For any position within the field of sports psychology, high school and college courses in psychology and health-related classes, as well as experience of some kind in sports is ideal, but there are great opportunities with varying levels of education required for those who don't envision a career working alongside athletes.

CORPORATE JOBS

Students who want to pursue a career in sports psychology, but who also have an interest in business, may be surprised to learn that there are jobs in the corporate world that are a good fit for someone with sports psychology training. Dedicated athletes who seek out the services of a sport psychologist have a lot in common with successful

Not all sports psychologists work with athletes. Some find themselves working in a corporate environment, helping others improve their health and achieve their personal fitness goals.

business executives: they are both very driven individuals who want to be the best at what they do. Business professionals with a competitive mindset may seek out guidance from someone who can help them achieve their goals in business as well as their personal fitness goals or things they wish to accomplish in a hobby sport. Some of these individuals will specifically seek out a licensed psychologist for this guidance, but others might prefer to work with someone whose education and experience leans more toward sports and health management. There are specific mental skills that in large part determine how successful an athlete will be. With the help of a trained professional, these same mental skills can be

NINE MENTAL SKILLS FOR SUCCESS

Successful athletes in virtually every sport share certain mental attributes. Some of these may come naturally to an athlete, while others must be cultivated. In his article "The Nine Mental Skills of Successful Athletes," Dr. Jack Lesyk, founder and director of the Ohio Center for Sports psychology, listed these nine mental skills used by successful athletes:

1. *Choose and maintain a positive attitude.*
2. *Maintain a high level of self-motivation.*
3. *Set high, realistic goals.*
4. *Deal effectively with people.*
5. *Use positive self-talk.*
6. *Use positive mental imagery.*
7. *Manage anxiety effectively.*
8. *Manage emotions effectively.*
9. *Maintain concentration.*

Dr. Lesyk believes athletes who possess all of these skills are more successful than those who do not. For non-athletes, working to strengthen these nine mental skills can still be of great benefit. Though it seems to be a simple, practical list, these nine skills are not easy to use consistently. A psychologist or mental coach can be instrumental in developing these skills and helping people achieve success on or off the field.

sharpened and used to achieve success in business as well as fitness. The combination of a solid background in sports and enough knowledge about psychology to understand how to motivate others is a valuable one, on or off the field.

A position within the human resources department of a large company is another option to consider for those trained in sports psychology who do not hold a license as a psychologist. Increasingly, large corporations are providing health services, incentives, and counseling in an effort to improve their employees' level of satisfaction, overall health, and job performance. In this type of position, the job duties might include talking with employees about health, fitness, and work-related goals; developing a plan for them; and giving them the motivation and tools necessary to follow through. Most positions of this type in the corporate arena require only a bachelor's degree and offer a great opportunity to help others realize their potential.

Though it is a business venture that requires a significant financial investment, some sports psychologists purchase or build their own gym or health and fitness club. Still others contract with fitness facilities to provide services as a performance enhancement consultant. Performance enhancement consultants may also be referred to as sport and exercise psychology consultants or mental coaches. These professionals are trained in sport and exercise but are not licensed

and more in demand, there will continue to be a growing need for sports psychologists interested in teaching. The number of colleges offering an undergraduate or advanced degree in sports psychology will increase as the number of students interested in the profession increases. There are many benefits of being a sport psychologist who teaches, including enjoying a set schedule corresponding with the academic calendar year, more job stability than sports psychologists who have to cultivate their own client lists, and the peace of mind of working at one location without being required to travel. Universities are often heavily involved

in research, especially as it relates to fields of study and

There are a growing number of opportunities, both at the high school and collegiate level, for those qualified to teach classes related to sports psychology.

degree programs they offer. Sports psychologists teaching at universities may have the chance to be involved in cutting-edge research, making contributions to the field that will bring notoriety and, most important, shape the future of the industry.

High school teaching positions for sports psychologists are relatively few and far between, but they are continuing to open up as a growing number of secondary schools strive to offer students career-related courses that give them an early advantage. Sports psychology in high school classrooms is an area that is poised for growth and one that will make a huge impact on future sports psychologists. Whereas many sports psychologists didn't even begin to learn about the field until their college years or beyond, increasingly, students will learn about this exciting career, gain inspiration from teachers who are sports psychologists, and begin laying the foundation for their own successful career as a sport psychologist while still in high school.

As is often the case, those in teaching positions may have a lower salary—albeit, a fairly secure one—than others in the field. There are ways for a sport psychologist to supplement a teaching salary, though. Many sports psychologists, recognizing the shortage of information available, choose to write one or more books about the field or an area of specialization within it. Others may choose to do some part-time consulting or mental coaching on the side, which not only brings in additional income, but also gives them the opportunity to gain practical experience and sharpen their counseling and coaching skills.

MILITARY JOBS

The expertise of sports psychologists has been sought out by branches of the military, and the demand is on the rise. The challenges and adversities faced by men and women in the military require both physical and mental strength and focus. The stakes are much higher than a win, a title, a medal, or a championship ring for these brave men and women, and giving them the best psychological support possible is not only in their best interest, it is in the best interest of their country and the people of any country they are sent to help.

Common stressors for military personnel include physical strain and fatigue, sleep deprivation, the very real threat of injury or death at any time, and the emotionally tough ordeal of being separated from their home and family members for prolonged periods of time. Traditionally, the military has had a treatment-based approach, reaching out to soldiers who were struggling with psychological issues. Military personnel have since come to realize that there is more benefit from an approach that seeks to prevent trauma, enhance psychological toughness, and encourage peak performance. This trend toward a more comprehensive, holistic approach that acknowledges the

Increasingly, sports psychologists are in demand in the military. Techniques that help athletes achieve peak performance are also highly effective in military training.

power of the mind is a huge step forward and has opened the door for sports psychologists interested in a military career.

At Fort Drum, New York, there is a successful training protocol in place for soldiers and their families. The program, called Comprehensive Soldier and Family Fitness, or CSF2, featuring a state of the art training center, complete with a team of educators, fitness and performance experts, and sports psychologists, is part of a larger initiative known as the army's Ready and Resilient Campaign. The program is unique both in its training methods and in its inclusion of military personnel's

THE HUMAN DIMENSION

In 2016, a battalion of army paratroopers at Fort Bragg, North Carolina, was one of the first groups of soldiers to be fully immersed in a program centered around mindfulness techniques as a method of improving fighting skills. Led by a sport psychologist, the soldiers engaged in relaxation exercises such as breath control and biofeedback in between machine gun training and other drills. The army called this new approach the Human Dimension and believe it helped their soldiers become agile, adaptive leaders, able to hone in on the task at hand and tune out distractions, under even the most intense circumstances, such as gunfire, sirens, explosions, and combat. Lieutenant Colonel Phil Kiniery made the decision to try this new training approach after meeting with a sport psychologist and learning about successful strategies used with athletes. The success of the Human Dimension approach has proved that techniques once reserved for Zen yoga masters or clinical psychologists have a place among elite fighting regiments.

family members. After all, a soldier's family faces many adversities common to military life right alongside their loved one, and the more stable a soldier's family members are, the better they can all nurture and support each other. At the CSF2 training center, psychologists teach people about the connection between mental toughness and physical performance. The result is soldiers, family members, and civilian employees who are more confident, more resilient, more physically fit, and are able to achieve improved performance in their jobs and training exercises. Fort Bragg's Jumpmaster Course is a shining example of the effectiveness of CSF2 techniques. Before CSF2, the average passing rate for the course was around 54 percent. Those who didn't pass had to repeat the course, which wasted valuable time and resources. After completing performance enhancement training through the CSF2 program, the average pass rate increased to an impressive 73 percent.

CSF2 came about on the heels of a first-of-its-kind study, funded by the army and conducted by a team of researchers and sports psychologists. Their aim was to determine successful military applications for cognitive techniques used by sports psychologists with elite athletes. The study included more than 2,400 recruits, divided into an active test group and a control group, and looked closely at six mental skills: mental skills foundations, goal setting, energy management, attention control, integrating imagery, and building confidence.

According to Coreen Harada, a consulting sport psychologist who took part in the study, the goal was

The army was the first branch of the military to conduct a scientific study that proved the cognitive techniques commonly used by sports psychologists are also effective in military applications.

to use those six mental skills to help soldiers improve their attitude, gain mental control over their physiological functions, focus on the task at hand, organize thoughts and set appropriate goals for each situation, and use psychological techniques such as visualization to complete tasks. Soldiers were taught to use these techniques in short sessions spread over ten weeks. An example of one of these training sessions included teaching goal setting, energy management, and attention control during a rifle marksmanship exercise. At the end of the session, recruits had learned to better control their heart rate and

In ancient Greece, foot races were one of the first athletic events ever held. The ancient Greeks believed in a strong mind-body connection long before the field of psychology emerged.

in turn, eventually paved the way for specific areas of specialization within the field of psychology to develop, with sports psychology getting its humble beginnings in the 1920s–1930s. As the field of psychology continued to emerge over the next several decades, so did the academic discipline of physical education. Over time, students of both psychology and physical education carved out a much-needed niche for sports psychologists.

THE STRUGGLES

Looking back, it's daunting to think about the many obstacles the field of sports psychology has overcome. Modern-day athletes and coaches realize that in order to be successful on the field, a strong, healthy mindset is essential, but the application of sports psychology principles wasn't always accepted or welcome on the field. For a long time, people were resistant to the idea of mental exercises that purported to make athletes run faster, throw farther, or jump higher. They were proponents of hard, physical work as a means to an end. Hard, physical work certainly is required of athletes, but for many years, the shortsighted belief that the level of an athlete's performance was simply a result of time spent in physical training prevailed. Thus, a poor performance meant the athlete needed more hours in the gym, and a great performance meant the athlete simply needed to keep up the good work.

Further hindering the growth of sports psychology as a field was a perceived stigma attached to psychological services. Athletes are taught to be tough—to play through pain, to push their physical limits, to rise up to the challenge of a great opponent. For a long time, most athletes were hesitant to disclose any mental health concerns or struggles for fear of being thought of as weak-minded and facing possible ridicule or rejection by teammates or coaches. This faulty thinking, in turn, often led athletes to become more anxious and depressed, making it difficult to excel in their sport. This stigma prevented the necessary recognition of athletes' mental struggles and the need for psychologists in the sports world.

Another stumbling block for sports psychology has been lack of funding in athletic departments, classrooms, and research efforts. Traditionally, when there has been no allotment for something, it is difficult to

As the stigma of seeking psychological help has diminished, the field of psychology has flourished and there is a growing demand for professional psychologists in all areas of specialty.

justify the new addition and make room for it in the budget. Adding a sport psychologist to a team's management staff, or an academic sport psychologist for teaching and research, requires a significant financial commitment. Many programs were hesitant to stretch the budget in this way while sports psychology was still an evolving profession on the cusp of acceptance. In addition, most universities have a counselor on staff in the school's student center. Making the case that sports psychology is a specialized area of study and that a sport psychologist is different than—but just as important as—a school's counselor continues to be difficult, especially at smaller schools with a tighter budget and fewer resources.

Finally, a lack of training models for psychologists, performance coaches, and mental health providers wishing to pursue a sports psychology career path contributed to a slow growth rate for the field. Students and professionals had very few resources to access in trying to increase their education in sports psychology. In the profession's earliest days, education and training in sports psychology had to be pieced together by dedicated, motivated, assertive individuals who were willing to do whatever was necessary to fill in the education and experience gaps and become effective sports psychologists. With very few schools offering graduate programs in sports psychology, many students pursued an advanced degree in psychology and then approached coaches, trainers, or other sports psychologists in hopes of landing an internship to gain the experience with athletes they needed. This is still a common path for sports psychology students, but thankfully there are more choices and much more guidance along the way now.

THE BREAKTHROUGHS

The late 1970s to the 1990s brought about important advancements in the field of sports psychology. It was

Since the 1980s when the US Olympic committee hired their first sports psychologists, there has been a steady increase in the presence of sports psychologists at each Olympic Games.

during this time that the gap between the science and the practice of sports psychology was bridged. During this time, some scientists began devoting their careers to research and advancement of sports psychology. In 1979, a new scientific journal called the *Journal of Sports psychology* began publication. Around the same time, there was increased interest in the field from the US Olympic Committee. In 1980, they developed a sports psychology advisory board and soon thereafter hired their first resident sport psychologist, followed by the appearance of the first sport psychologist at an Olympic Games. In 1985, the Association for the Advancement of Applied Sports psychology (AAASP) was formed. (Since then, the "Advancement" has been dropped from the name and it is now the AASP). This association focuses heavily on using psychological methodologies to help athletes excel in their sports environments and is the largest applied sports psychology organization in the world. The American Psychological Association formed Division 47 in 1986. This new division, devoted specifically to sports psychology, continues to provide guidance, networking, and learning opportunities for students, professionals, and athletes. In 1991, the AASP implemented its Certified Consultant designation, a prestigious qualification that is awarded to those at the top of their field. Additional journals dedicated to sports psychology soon began publication, including the *Sport Psychologist* (1986) and the *Journal of Applied Sports psychology* (1989). Suddenly, there were a growing number of practitioners consulting with coaches and athletes, and by the year 2000, there was a large, established research field, a wealth of information and professional conferences, and several academic degree programs available.

THE OUTLOOK

Sports psychology had an uphill battle gaining footing as a recognized field. Today a career as a sport psychologist

A NEW GENERATION OF ATHLETES

Most coaches, even those involved in youth sports, have a burning desire to win. While winning is an exciting and enjoyable experience for players, parents, fans, and coaches alike, these days, many coaches are placing just as much emphasis on educating this new generation of athletes as winning. In Newton, Massachusetts, the Lasell College men's basketball team coaches, Mitch Lyons and Chris Harvey, believed in the importance of educating student-athletes about the psychology of sports in order to help them learn valuable life skills. They adopted a Massachusetts high school initiative that uses a written curriculum and text that all players and coaches must read and study. This new sports-team model teaches young athletes to use sports as a vehicle for sharpening mental skills and learning to be successful both on and off the field. The curriculum provides exercises built around concepts such as positive thinking, actively helping and encouraging others, concentrating fully on the requirements of a task rather than the outcome, recognizing and changing negative thoughts, visualizing success, using meditation to relax, and setting daily goals. At Lasell College, the coaches were very encouraged by what they saw. Their players enjoyed increased self-confidence and improvements both on and off the court. The initiative has since expanded to other schools, and participating coaches all hold a shared belief that it is a matter of national interest to instill confidence and critical thinking skills in the leaders of tomorrow. These are skills that will be beneficial to the players in all aspects of their lives, and as an added bonus, participating in this program often leads to a win on the court as well!

continues to be a challenging pursuit in many regards, but thanks to forward-thinking scientists and researchers and the spirit that drives people to push themselves to be the best they can be, there is a bright future ahead for the sports psychologists of tomorrow. Universities and athletic programs at all levels are hiring sports psychologists in increasing numbers. High school teaching jobs are opening up, as well as opportunities in the corporate world. According to the American Psychological Association, the United States Army is a leading employer of sports psychologists. The demand for master's and doctorate-

As interest in the field of sports psychology grows, so will the demand for professionals in the field who are interested in conducting research and teaching.

level graduates who can help soldiers learn to perform well under pressure is only expected to rise. There are many sports psychologists in private practice, consulting with individuals on all aspects of performance-related psychological training.

The surge in popularity of the sports psychology field was apparent by the attendance of more than seven hundred delegates from seventy countries at the 2009 World Congress of Sports psychology conference, held in Morocco. Hundreds of research studies are now being conducted every year, and the number of universities offering sports psychology specializations at the graduate level has seen a sharp increase. It is safe to say contemporary sport and exercise psychology is firmly established and here to stay. Positive changes are coming about in the field, because of the irrefutable evidence of its effectiveness, the fading away of the antiquated notion that seeking psychological help equates to weakness, and the tremendous interest and growth in the research and application of clinical and applied psychological methodologies. The explosion of interest in the field has also been fueled by a disturbing rise in obesity rates and a decline in physical activity in Western countries. As media outlets and social networking shine more light on the benefits of sports psychology, the number of Olympians, professional athletes, collegiate athletic programs, youth athletic programs, and recreational athletes using the services of a sport

Sports psychologists inspire individuals to achieve their goals, realize their dreams, and perform their best. It is a challenging career but one that is extremely rewarding on many levels.

psychologist will continue to increase. The relationship between mental and physical health has garnered considerable interest and continues to highlight the need for qualified sport and exercise psychologists who can help optimize overall health for everyone seeking a more successful, stronger, longer, happier life.

Though projections specific to the sports psychology area of specialization are not listed, the Bureau of Labor Statistics predicts an increase of 32,500 jobs in the field of psychology between 2014 and 2024. This represents a much faster-than-average job increase, at 19 percent, and bodes well for students embarking on any area of specialization within psychology. All factors considered, it can reasonably be assumed that the field of sports psychology is a challenging one that requires an above-average level of academic achievement and experience to excel in, but one that will continue to expand and offer exciting, lucrative, rewarding job opportunities for those who meet the requirements.

COLLEGE AND UNIVERSITY SPORTS PSYCHOLOGY PROGRAMS

Drexel University
Admissions Center
Main Building, Room 212, 2nd
   Floor
3141 Chestnut Street
Philadelphia, PA 19104
(215) 895-2400
http://www.drexel.edu
Programs of study: sport
   management, psychology

Florida State University
A2500 University Center
PO Box 3062400
Tallahassee, FL 32306-2400
(850) 644-6200
https://www.fsu.edu
Programs of study: sports
   psychology

Fredonia State University
Admissions Office
Fenner House
178 Central Avenue
Fredonia, NY 14063
(716) 673-3251
http://home.fredonia.edu
Programs of study: sport and
   exercise psychology

Laurentian University
Laurentian University
   Admissions
935 Ramsey Lake Road
Sudbury, ON P3E 2C6
Canada
 (705) 675-1151
https://laurentian.ca
Programs of study: human
   kinetics, kinesiology, sports
   psychology, sport and physical education, psychology

Minnesota State University-
   Mankato
Office of Admissions
122 Taylor Center
Mankato, MN 56001
(507) 389-1822
https://www.mnsu.edu
Programs of study: sport and
   exercise psychology

National University
National University Academic
  Headquarters
11255 North Torrey Pines Road
La Jolla, CA 92037
(215) 628-8648
https://www.nu.edu
Programs of study: sports
  psychology

Purdue University
Purdue University Office of
  Admissions
Schleman Hall of Student
  Services
475 Stadium Mall Drive
West Lafayette, IN 47907-2050
(765) 494-1776
http://www.purdue.edu
Programs of study: sport and
  exercise psychology

Queens University
School of Kinesiology and
  Health Studies
SKHS Building, KHS 206
28 Division Street
Kingston, ON K7L 3N6
Canada
(613) 533-2666
http://www.queensu.ca/skhs
Programs of study: kinesiology,
  health studies, physical and
  health education, psychology
  of sport and physical activity

Southern Illinois University
Student Services Building
1263 Lincoln Drive
Carbondale, IL 62901
(618) 536-4405
http://siu.edu
Programs of study: exercise and
  sports psychology

Texas Christian University
TCU Office of Admission
TCU Box 297013
Fort Worth, Texas 76129
(817) 257-7490
http://www.tcu.edu
Programs of study: psychosocial
  kinesiology

University of Utah
Office of Admissions
201 S 1460 E, Room 250 S
Salt Lake City, UT 84112
(801) 581-8761
https://www.utah.edu
Programs of study: kinesiology,
  sport and exercise psychology

West Virginia University
Office of Admissions
PO Box 6009
One Waterfront Place
Morgantown, WV 26506-6009
(304) 293-2121
https://www.wvu.edu
Programs of study: counseling,
  sport and exercise psychology

SPORTS PSYCHOLOGISTS

ACADEMICS

Bachelor's degree

Master's degree

Doctoral degree (for positions requiring licensure as a psychologist)

AASP or ABSP Certification (for positions requiring sport psychology certification)

EXPERIENCE

Volunteer with youth sports organizations

Participate in sports as an athlete, coach, or manager

Internships in psychology and/or sports

CAREER PATHS

Many sports psychologists work directly with athletes.

Health and fitness consulting is also an option.

Teaching and research at the high school or college level is another option.

Many sports psychologists work with members of the military.

RESPONSIBILITIES

Identify and treat individuals with performance-related
psychological problems

Motivate individuals to achieve peak performance

Treat individuals with post-performance issues such as injury,
depression, or trauma

Research and teaching (for those pursuing sports psychology educational
fields)

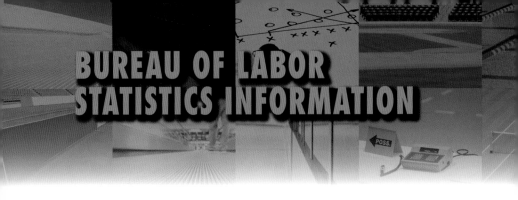

PSYCHOLOGIST

What psychologists do—Psychologists study cognitive, emotional, and social processes and behavior by observing, interpreting, and recording how people relate to one another and their environments. *Sports psychologists specialize in using psychological strategies to help athletes achieve peak performance.

Work environment—Some psychologists work independently conducting research, consulting with clients, or working with patients. Others work as part of a health care team collaborating with physicians and social workers, or in school settings working with students, teachers, parents, and other educators. Those in private practice often work evenings and weekends to accommodate clients. *Sports psychologists often work directly with athletes, coaches, and athletic training staff.

How to become a psychologist—Although psychologists typically need a doctoral degree in psychology, a master's degree is sufficient for some positions. Psychologists in independent practice also need a license. *Sports psychologists may or may not need a license, depending on their specific place of employment.

Job outlook—Employment of psychologists is projected to grow 19 percent from 2014 to 2024, much faster than the average for all occupations. Job prospects should be best for those who have a doctoral degree in an applied specialty.

anxiety A feeling of worry and nervousness, often about an upcoming event.

bachelor's degree A college degree in a specific course of study, typically awarded approximately four years after starting college; also called an undergraduate degree.

cognitive Relating to the mind processes involved in thinking, experiencing, or sensing things.

cognitive behavioral therapy (CBT) A type of psychological treatment aimed at changing faulty patterns of thinking or behavior.

control group A group in an experiment or study that does not receive treatment and is used for comparison purposes to measure the test subjects' results.

department chair The head of a college department.

depression Intense feelings of sadness and dejection, often requiring counseling from a mental health professional.

doctoral degree The highest level of academic degree.

dual credit classes Classes taken in high school that offer two types of credit simultaneously: high school course credit and college course credit.

extracurricular Relating to school activities that take place outside of regular school hours.

graduate program An academic program at a college or university that offers an advanced degree such as a master's degree or doctoral degree.

interdisciplinary Relating to more than just one branch of knowledge or training.

master's degree An advanced college degree typically awarded after a bachelor's degree has been earned and two additional years of specific courses have been completed.

performance anxiety Anxiety an athlete might feel right before taking the field, court, or ring.

post-traumatic stress disorder (PTSD) A persistent condition of mental and emotional distress that occurs as a result of an incidence of severe injury or psychological shock.

prodigies People with exceptional qualities, talents, or abilities in a particular area.

psychology The science of behavior and the mind that attempts to help and better understand people by studying their mental processes, thoughts, and experiences.

social facilitation The tendency of people to perform differently when they are in the presence of others than when they are alone; also referred to as "the audience effect."

social science Subject matter or courses related to the scientific study of human society and social relationships.

sport psychologist A professional in the field of psychology who uses psychological knowledge and skills to help athletes overcome mental and physical challenges and reach their highest potential.

test group A group in an experiment or study that receives treatment and whose outcomes are measured to determine the effectiveness of the treatment.

thesis A long essay involving extensive research completed by a student as part of the requirement for earning a degree.

visualization A psychological method in which the person uses their imagination to recreate all aspects of an event, including imagining sights, sounds, and feelings related to the event.

FOR MORE INFORMATION

American Board of Sports psychology (ABSP)

McLean Hospital, Mailstop 327

115 Mill Street

Belmont, MA 02478

Website: http://americanboardofsportpsychology.org

Facebook: @AmericanBoardOfSportPsychology

Twitter: @A_B_S_P_

This organization's mission is the advancement of practice, education, and training in applied sports psychology. The website provides information about internships, fellowships, and requirements for professional certification through ABSP as a sport psychologist.

American Psychological Association Division 47 (APA47)

750 First Street NE

Washington, DC 20002-4242

(202) 336-5500

Website: http://www.apadivisions.org/division-47/index
.aspx

Facebook: @APADivision47

Twitter: @APADivision47

This website is a wealth of information, offering several levels of membership and opportunities for students and professionals. This organization is committed to providing the latest in research and development news in the field and promoting best practices in psychology and the sport sciences.

Association for Applied Sports psychology (AASP)

8365 Keystone Crossing, Suite 107

Indianapolis, IN 46240

(317) 205-9225

Website: http://www.appliedsportpsych.org

Facebook: @AssociationforAppliedSportPsychology

Twitter: @AASPTweets

This is an international multidisciplinary organization that promotes the development of ethical practice in sports psychology and offers certification to highly qualified sports psychologists. The website offers information about membership, conferences, publications, scholarships, and awards.

Canadian Psychological Association (CPA)

Laurier Avenue West, Suite 702

Ottawa, ON K1P 5J3

Canada

(613) 237-2144

Website: http://www.cpa.ca/aboutcpa/cpasections /sportandexercise

Facebook: @CPA.SCP

Twitter: @CPA.SCP

The Canadian Psychological Association promotes the advancement and development of psychological knowledge and practices to improve the health and well-being of all Canadians. The Sport and Psychology branch of the organization specifically supports students and professionals in Canada in the field of sport and exercise psychology. They welcome all individuals interested in sport and exercise psychology and offer different levels of membership, an informative annual convention, and ongoing support services.

International Mental Game Coaching Association (IMGCA)

PO Box 8151

San Jose, CA 95155

(408) 440-2398

Website: http://www.mentalgamecoaching.com

This organization supports the research, development, and growth of mental game coaching. The website provides general information for those interested in sports performance, health, fitness, and stress management. The organization's president and founder has served as a mental game coach to thousands of athletes at all levels, from junior high students to Olympians.

Psychologists' Association of Alberta

Unit 103, 1207-91 Street SW

Edmonton, AB T6X 1E9

Canada

(780) 424-0294

Website: https://www.psychologistsassociation.ab.ca

Twitter: @PAAlberta

This organization provides information about careers in psychology as well as a list of educational programs in psychology in Canada.

University of North Texas Center for Sports psychology

1611 West Mulberry Street

Room 235, Terrill Hall

Denton, TX 76203

(940) 369-7767

Website: https://sportpsych.unt.edu

Twitter: @UNTSportPsych

This organization supports the research, development, and teaching of sports psychology. The website provides information about current research projects, grants, and educational opportunities for coaches and future sports psychologists.

WEBSITES

Because of the changing nature of internet links, Rosen Publishing has developed an online list of websites related to the subject of this book. This site is updated regularly. Please use this link to access the list:

http://www.rosenlinks.com/GCSI/Psych

FOR FURTHER READING

Afremow, Jim. *The Champion's Mind: How Great Athletes Think, Train, and Thrive.* Emmaus, PA: Rodale Books, 2015.

Bilas, Jay. *Toughness: Developing True Strength On and Off the Court.* New York, NY: New American Library, 2014.

Calipari, John. *Players First: Coaching from the Inside Out.* New York, NY: Penguin, 2014.

Cohen, Rhonda. *Sports psychology: The Basics: Optimising Human Performance.* London, UK: Bloomsbury Sport, 2016.

Divine, Mark. *The Way of the Seal: Think Like an Elite Warrior to Lead and Succeed.* White Plains, NY: Reader's Digest Association, 2016.

Donnelly, Darrin. *Think Like a Warrior: The Five Inner Beliefs That Make You Unstoppable.* Lenexa, KS: Shamrock New Media, 2016.

Eccles, CJ. *What Is Sports psychology?* Seattle, WA: Amazon Digital Services, 2016.

Ehrmann, Joe, and Gregory Jordan. *Inside Out Coaching: How Sports Can Transform Lives.* New York, NY: Simon & Schuster, 2011.

Epstein, David. *The Sports Gene: Inside the Science of Extraordinary Athletic Performance.* New York, NY: Penguin Random House, 2013.

Fitzgerald, Matt. *How Bad Do You Want It?: Mastering the Psychology of Mind Over Muscle.* Boulder, CO: Velo Press, 2015.

Gordon, John, and Mike Smith. *You Win in the Locker Room First.* Hoboken, NJ: Wiley, 2015.

Grover, Tim S. *Relentless: From Good to Great to Unstoppable.* New York, NY: Scribner, 2014.

LaBella, Laura. *Dream Jobs in Sports Fitness and Medicine* (Great Careers in the Sports Industry). New York, NY: Rosen, 2013.

Mumford, George. *The Mindful Athlete: Secrets to Pure Performance.* Berkeley, CA: Parallax Press, 2016.

Perry, John. *Sports Psychology—A Complete Introduction* (Teach Yourself). London, UK: Hodder Education, 2016.

Phelps, Michael. *Beneath the Surface: My Story.* New York, NY: Skyhorse Publishing, 2013.

Rooney, Anne. *The History of Psychology* (The History of the Humanities and Social Sciences). New York, NY: Rosen, 2017.

Rotella, Bob. *How Champions Think: In Sports and in Life.* New York, NY: Simon & Schuster, 2015.

Selk, Jason. *10-Minute Toughness: The Mental Training Program for Winning Before the Game Begins. Developing True Strength On and Off the Court.* Columbus, OH: McGraw Hill Education, 2008.

Sheard, Michael. *Mental Toughness: The Mindset Behind Sporting Achievement.* Second edition. London, UK: Taylor and Francis Books, 2012.

Smith, Ronald E., and Frank L. Smoll. *Sports psychology for Youth Coaches: Developing Champions in Sports and Life.* Lanham, MD: Rowman and Littlefield Publishers, 2012.

Wolframm, Inga. *Perfect Mind: Perfect Ride: Sports psychology for Successful Riding.* Shrewsbury, UK: Kenilworth Press, 2015.

BIBLIOGRAPHY

Baxter, Brian. "2014—the Year of Sports psychology?" Sports psychology Institute Northwest, April 23, 2014. http://spinw.com/2014/04/2014-the-year-of-sport
-psychology/.

Burke, Kevin L. "What Do Athletes Mean by 'Playing in the Zone?'" *Sporting News Media*, January 26, 2017. http://www.sportingnews.com/other-sports/news /what-does-in-the-zone-mean-athletes-peak -performances/1kugz4tuad8j513rgnpophp65q.

Campbell, Rich. "6 Ways High School Students Can Prepare for Careers in Sports." The Balance, August 30, 2016. https://www.thebalance.com/high-school -students-prepare-for-sports-careers-3113321.

"A Career in Sport and Performance Technology." American Psychological Association, 2017. Retrieved March 1, 2017. http://www.apa.org/action/science /performance/education-training.aspx.

Clarey, Christopher. "Olympians Use Imagery as Mental Training." *New York Times*, February 22, 2014. https:// www.nytimes.com/2014/02/23/sports/olympics/olym-pians-use-imagery-as-mental-training.html?_r=0.

Cole, Bill. "Why Are Some Athletes Reluctant to Use Sports Psychologists?" "Resistance to Sports Psychology." William B. Cole Consultants, 2017. http://www.mentalgamecoach.com/articles /ResistanceToSportsPsychology.html.

Dahlkoetter, Dr. JoAnn. "Sochi Olympics and Sports

Psychology for Athletes." *Huffington Post*, February 10, 2014. http://www.huffingtonpost.com/dr-joann -dahlkoetter/sochi-olympics_b_4582950.html.

"Dr. Sean Richardson." CareersinPsychology.org. Retrieved March 5, 2017. http://careersinpsychology .org/interview/dr-sean-richardson/.

Kennedy, Michelle. "Comprehensive Soldier, Family Fitness Uses Sports Psychology to Enhance Performance." Army.mil, December 2, 2013. https:// www.army.mil/article/116183/Comprehensive _Soldier__Family_Fitness_uses_sports_psychology _to_enhance_performance.

Lesyk, Jack J. "The Nine Mental Skills of Successful Athletes." Ohio Center for Sports psychology, 1998. Retrieved March 10, 2017. https://www.sportpsych .org/nine-mental-skills-overview.

Lyons, Mitch. "Education World: Soapbox: Sports-Psychology Curriculum Focuses on Educating Athletes and Winning." Education World. Retrieved March 20, 2017. http://www.educationworld.com /a_issues/soapbox/soapbox005.shtml.

McGee, Ryan. "120,000 Ways to Die." ESPN, July 13, 2012. http://www.espn.com/action/story/_/id /8133299/base-jumper-felix-baumgartner-free -fall-space-espn-magazine.

Price, Jay. "Army Embraces Psychology, Zen Traditions to Train Paratroopers." American Homefront Project, July 6, 2016. http://americanhomefront.wunc.org /post/army-embraces-psychology-zen-traditions -train-paratroopers.

"Psychologists: Summary." US Bureau of Labor Statistics, December 17, 2015. https://www.bls.gov/ooh /life-physical-and-social-science/psychologists.htm.

Rathi, Akshat. "What Sports Psychologists Do for Olympic Athletes That Coaches Can't." Quartz, August 9, 2016. https://qz.com/753857 /for-olympians-to-reach-the-highest-level-they -need-a-sports-psychologist/.

Shapiro, John Florio and Ouisie. "The Dark Side of Going for Gold." *Atlantic*, August 18, 2016. https:// www.theatlantic.com/health/archive/2016/08 /post-olympic-depression/496244/.

"Summer Programs in Psychology for High School Students." American Psychological Association, 2017. Retrieved March 5, 2017. http://www.apa.org /science/resources/summer-student-programs.aspx.

Tartakovsky, Margarita. "Sports psychology and Its History." World of Psychology, May 24, 2016. http://psychcentral.com/blog/archives/2011/07/15 /sport-psychology-and-its-history/.

"The True Measure of Doug McDermott." ABC News, March 6, 2014. http://abcnews.go.com/Sports /true-measure-doug-mcdermott/story?id=22798130.

Vergun, David. "Mental Skills Training Improving Soldier Performance." Army.mil, August 3, 2015. https://www.army.mil/article/153231/Mental_skills _training_improving_Soldier_performance/.

INDEX

ABOUT THE AUTHOR

Jessica Shaw has a BA in psychology from Texas State University. She has worked in human services and taught preschool. She currently writes nonfiction, fiction, and poetry for children and young adults, including standardized testing material and work appearing in numerous children's publications.

PHOTO CREDITS

Cover, p. 1 Prostock Studio/Shutterstock.com; cover, p. 1 (background) Adam Friedberg/The Image Bank /Getty Images; p. 4 Peter Bischoff/PB Archive /Getty Images; pp. 9, 22–23, 80–81, 82–83 Monkey Business Images /Shutterstock.com; p. 11 Richard Cavalleri/Shutterstock.com; p. 13 Tomwang112/iStock/Thinkstock; pp. 14-15 Pete Saloutos/Image Source /Getty Images; pp. 18–19 Chris Hondros/Getty Images; pp. 24, 38–39 asiseeit /E+/Getty Images; pp. 28–29 Torwaistudio/Shutterstock.com; p. 30 Larry St.Pierre/Shutterstock.com; pp. 34–35 Portland Press Herald/Getty Images; pp. 40–41, 52–53 Aspen Photo/Shutterstock.com; pp. 44–45 Cultura RM Exclusive/Frank and Helena/Getty Images; pp. 48–49 Joseph Sohm /Shutterstock.com; p. 55 © AP Images; pp. 60–61 Aykut Erdogdu/Shutterstock .com; pp. 64–65 Antonin Thuillier/AFP/Getty Images; pp. 70–71 Bettmann /Getty Images; pp. 72–73 ullstein bild/Getty Images; pp. 76–77 Dima Sidelnikov/iStock/Thinkstock; pp. 86–87 Scott Olson/Getty Images; pp. 90–91 Patrick Robert-Corbis/Corbis Historical/Getty Images; p. 94 Private Collection/The Stapleton Collection/Bridgeman Images; p. 96 AlexRaths /iStock/Thinkstock; pp. 98–99 PA Images Archive/Getty Images; p. 102 monkeybusinessimages/iStock/Thinkstock; p. 104 Yellow Dog Productions /Iconica/Getty Images; interior design elements: © www.istockphoto.com / hudiemm (grid pattern); http://lostandtaken.com (striped border); pp. 8, 21, 37, 55, 75, 93, 106, 108, 110, 111, 114, 118, 121, 124 (montage) © www .iStockphoto.com, Shutterstock.com.

Designer: Brian Garvey: Layout Designer: Ellina Litmanovich; Editor: Bethany Bryan; Photo Researcher: Sherri Jackson